SEAFARERS
OF THE GULF

**Written and photographed
by Shirley Kay**

D0652950

Published with
the support and
encouragement of

**DUBAI PORTS
AUTHORITY**

MOTIVATE
PUBLISHING

Published by Motivate Publishing

Dubai: PO Box 2331, Dubai, UAE
Tel: (04) 824060, Fax: (04) 824436

Abu Dhabi: PO Box 43072, Abu Dhabi, UAE
Tel: (02) 311666, Fax: (02) 311888

UK: London House, 26/40, Kensington High
Street, London W8 4PF
Tel: (071) 938 2222, Fax: (071) 937 7293

Directors:
Obaid Humaid Al Tayer
Ian Fairservice

First published 1992
Reprinted 1994

ISBN 1 873544 38 3

Printed by Emirates Printing Press, Dubai

CONTENTS

The palm-frond shasha is the most ancient of boat designs in use in the Gulf.

MOST ANCIENT OF ROUTES

"Ships of Meluhha, ships of Magan and ships of Dilmun (he made) tie up alongside the quay of Agad."
Tablet of King Sargon of Agad

The long narrow waterway of the Gulf is a sea on which men dared to venture from the very earliest times. The waters are shallow all along the Arabian shores, and sandbank islands provide shelter or respite from the waves. Even the smallest and most primitive of craft might reach its destination safely by hugging the Arabian shoreline.

The world's earliest civilisation developed in the lands at the head of the Gulf, in Mesopotamia between the twin rivers of the Tigris and the Euphrates, the land which is now Iraq. There, from about 5000 BC, enterprising city states were developed near the southern marshlands by people known as the Sumerians. They planted great grain fields on the river silt and became rich enough to build splendid temples of mud bricks, the only building material available in their river valley land. By 3000 BC they had invented the art of writing, initially in order to keep the accounts of their increasingly wealthy temples.

They lived in a world where grain grew easily on the sun-baked mud flats, and where flocks could graze and increase. But they lacked many of the raw materials of well-developed city life — they had no stone for example, no wood, and no metals — so they set out in search of the goods they lacked. To the north and east they could travel overland, but towards the south lay the Gulf and the maritime routes to the east.

The Sumerians, as river people, must from early times have launched out onto the waters. They had no wood for boats but they did have magnificent reeds growing high in their marshes. These reeds, if cut in the month of August, will float, though

5

they soon become waterlogged if cut at any other season of the year. Five-thousand-year-old models of reed boats coated in pitch have been found in Sumeria, and the oldest Sumerian written sign for 'boat' was a picture of a sickle-shaped reed boat. Quite early, too, they must have found the advantage of a sail, which would allow a following wind to propel the boat across the waters. A clay model of a boat was found in a Sumerian grave.

Such little boats, of course, would be fine on the rivers and marshes. But could they really have been used on the open sea? Thor Heyerdahl built a large reed boat on Sumerian lines and launched it on the Tigris in 1977. He was able to sail it down the Gulf, and around Arabia to arrive eventually in Djibouti on the Red Sea coast of Africa, without the assistance of any modern aids to sailing at all.

Along the coasts of what is now the UAE and Oman, rather similar small boats were built of an equivalent local material, palm fronds. These boats are known as 'shashas', and they are still to be found along the east coast, especially in the Kalba area. Traditionally they were made only of the products of the palm tree, the spines of the fronds making the hull and deck of the boat, the fibrous stumps of the fronds providing the buoyancy below the deck, and the fibres of the tree, wound into cords, being used to tie the fronds together. Today, polystyrene replaces the palm stumps, and nylon is used instead of the palm cords, but basically the boat is as it has been for thousands of years. Local fishermen still rate it a good craft for a single sailor, or two at most.

The pottery of Al Ubaid

Al Ubaid was one of the earliest Sumerian towns, lying on the Euphrates plain not far away from the great cities of Ur and Eridu. Today all that is left of those fabled cities is a high mound of earth rising from a desolate, dust-bowl plain, now far removed from the Euphrates, which gave them life but which has frequently altered its course.

In ancient times, though, some 6 or 7,000 years ago, they were the world's leading cities, hungry for imported luxuries with which to adorn their temples. For many centuries the people of these towns made a recognisable type of pottery, greenish or beige with black or brown designs painted on it, called Al Ubaid pottery — from the place where it was first found. Pottery was a luxury in those days, and was also of course very breakable.

So when amateur archaeologists claimed that they were finding small pieces of Al Ubaid pottery along the east coast of Saudi Arabia, few believed them. But they pursued their quest, finding hundreds of potsherds on some sites, and eventually it was accepted that amazingly, 6,000-year-old pottery from distant Sumeria was littered on sand dunes in Arabia, among a scatter of flint tools and broken sea shells.

For many years this pottery was only found in Saudi Arabia, where it might have come by land. But then at last similar potsherds were found in

Sandy shores and shallow seas of the Gulf made sailing easy from the earliest times.

Above: Al Ubaid pottery, like this jar from the great Sumerian city of Ur, was exported along the Gulf. Right: A 5,000-year-old model of a boat from north of Sumeria.
(Courtesy Ashmolean Museum, Oxford)

Bahrain, Qatar and recently in the UAE. The pottery is on, or not far from the coast and so must almost surely have been brought by boat. Some of the pieces show signs of careful repair — clearly they could not readily be replaced.

This pottery just might have been made locally in all those places, a copy of the desirable bowls from the north. But when the small pieces found in distant places were analysed by scientific methods (neutron activation) it was shown that all were made of the clays of Sumeria, all had been exported along the Gulf from their homeland. And already on these most ancient Gulf sites there were flints brought from Anatolia (central Turkey) and an occasional bead of carnelian or amazonite from India.

Indus to Dilmun

Although Sumeria had a head start on any other civilisation in the world, in the centuries around 3000 BC another notable riverside civilisation arose in the Indus Valley, in the region that is now Pakistan. There, great cities were built at Harappa and Mohenjo Daro, cities which each covered an area of several hundred hectares. Huge granaries were the main feature of their citadels and they had need of imported goods from abroad. The two civilisations complemented each other; each could provide for the other's requirements.

So by 2500 BC or thereabouts, a flourishing trade developed between these distant places, a trade which was carried by ship along the length of the Gulf. It was carried and organised by seafarers of the Gulf in a great maritime trading operation which was centred on Dilmun, the ancient name for the islands of Bahrain and neighbouring seaboard of Arabia as well.

This trade is particularly fascinating since so many of the goods which travelled along the route have been found at 'stopping places' along the way. The old ports of Oman, UAE, Bahrain, Saudi Arabia and Failaka (off Kuwait), have all produced objects made in the Indus Valley, in the highlands of Iran, in the other Gulf states and occasionally in Sumeria.

Oddly though, much less has been found from Sumeria, the fount of the Gulf's maritime trade, than might be expected. Sumeria's exports were largely perishable: grain, dates, vegetable oils, skins and textiles. But the Sumerians marked their bales of goods with a seal mark impressed in clay, and the marks of their characteristic cylinder seals have been found on clay sealings and potsherds from one end of the route to the other, along with the occasional seal itself. Some of the seal impressions show reed boats, with high bow and stern, of the kind made thousands of years later for the long sea voyage in 1977 by Thor Heyerdahl.

Exports from the Indus, known to the Sumerians as Meluhha, were more durable: carnelian beads, lapis lazuli, gold and silver, ivory and wood. They too used seals to mark their goods and these sealing marks, often with pictures of hump-backed bulls but sometimes with more exotic fauna — elephants, tigers, crocodiles and the like — have also been found on ancient sites.

Much is known of the Gulf's sea trade more than 4,000 years ago, thanks to the thousands of little clay tablets impressed with the reed marks of ancient cuneiform writing which have been found in so many Sumerian cities. These tablets tell especially of the trade with Dilmun: they relate how the shipwrights of Dilmun imported wood for their ships, how ships from Dilmun came up to their quays on the banks of the Tigris and Euphrates, how merchants from Dilmun transported their goods. A tablet of 2500 BC tells of ships from Dilmun bringing wood from far places to Lagash in Sumeria, another of 2300 BC tells how King Sargon of Agad made "ships of Meluhha, ships of Magan and ships of Dilmun tie up alongside the quay of Agad".

Dilmun, or Bahrain as we now know it, flourished on this entrepot trade. Its main port on the north coast, at the site of the Bahrain fort, grew into a sizeable mound as one generation of buildings

Dilmun stamp seal showing ancient boat.
(Courtesy Ministry of Information, Bahrain)

Excavations on the mound of Tell Abraq near the coast of Umm Al Quwain.

succeeded another. Its main temple at Barbar, not far away, was an impressive building of well-cut stone columns covered in copper sheeting, built on the lines of the temple of Al Ubaid. And throughout the island some 150,000 burial mounds were piled up over well-made stone-lined graves.

The Sumerians regarded Dilmun, with its fresh water springs and green palm groves, as a paradise island and many of their legends were sited there. "Then Ziusudra the King, the preserver of vegetation and of the seed of mankind, in the land of the crossing, in the land of Dilmun, the place where the sun rises, they (the gods) caused to dwell," runs a Sumerian version of the great flood story.

But the people of Dilmun were hard-headed businessmen as well and occasional Sumerian clay tablets complain of unduly sharp business deals, though for the most part trade seems to have run smoothly. The Dilmun merchants developed their own stamp seals to mark their goods — small, round, button-shaped seals with a picture cut on the smooth face, and a curved back decorated with circles with a dot in the middle. The pictures show legendary scenes, two men drinking through straws from a large flask, a hero sitting by the tree of life, or gazelles, scorpions, bulls, and even boats. These ancient pictures of boats show small and simple craft with curved bow and stern, a mast and apparently side oars for rudders.

A distant mirror

On the trade route between the Indus and Bahrain lay the land of Magan, whose boats were mentioned in the Agad tablet quoted above, and in many others. Magan was a land of ship-builders in the Sumerian texts, and above all it was a land of copper, the land of the copper mountain. In recent years archaeologists have shown that Magan must have been Oman and the UAE, the land of the Hajar Mountains with their many ancient copper mines.

In the ancient world, copper was the earliest functional metal to be worked. Gold and silver were prized above all for ornament, but it was copper, or the copper/tin alloy of bronze which was used for tools, weapons and tableware. Ownership of a copper mine 4,000 years ago was the equivalent of ownership of an oil well today. It brought wealth, a rising standard of living, and the leisure to create works of art and to import luxury goods.

Many ancient copper workings have been found in the Hajar Mountains, some of the biggest of them in Wadi Jizzi which runs from the Buraimi oasis through to the coast of Oman. Thousands of tons of black slag mark the sites where the copper was smelted. Copper wealth enabled the inhabitants of the oasis to build magnificent tombs, like the fine one in Hili gardens. Here huge slabs of stone were brought from the mountains a couple of kilometres away, and lively scenes of men and animals were carved in relief on the slabs which were then set upright to cover the tomb.

Similar tombs were found on the island of Umm an Nar, near Abu Dhabi, alongside a well-built stone settlement. So arid and unpromising as a settlement site is this island that it must surely have served as the port from which copper was exported, while imports found on the island include a pot from Baluchistan, and a seal impression from Sumeria. Some of the pots made at Umm an Nar itself have been found in graves in Bahrain.

For several hundred years the trade in Magan's copper continued to flow along the Gulf, and eastwards as far as the Indus. In the north of the UAE a jar and a stone weight from Harappa were found in a grave near Ras Al Khaimah, while in another grave in the same area was a piece of a jar from Dilmun. Another Harappan stone weight was found in the ruins of a great tower, built well over 4,000 years ago on the coast near Umm Al Quwain and inhabited for hundreds of years.

Doorway of the great tomb at Hili.

Furnaces of an ancient copper mine in Wadi Jizzi.

This anchor of Roman times survived as a building stone.

GREEKS AND ROMANS

"It is from these trees that the aromatic substance known as incense is extracted."

Sindbad the Sailor

The heyday of the very ancient trade routes along the Gulf came to an end around 1800 BC with the collapse of the Indus civilisation. Their great cities were gradually reduced to mounds of ruins, the result of invasion or flood or plague perhaps — a mystery that has not yet been solved. Maritime trade of the lower Gulf diminished after this, although trade in the northern Gulf, between Bahrain and Mesopotamia, continued to flow.

However, the Gulf was never forgotten as the highway to the east. When the extraordinary Greek leader, Alexander the Great, conquered Persia and led his armies east to the banks of the Indus River, one of his aims was to find a sea route to command the valuable trade in spices and incense coming from eastern Arabia and countries beyond. In 323 BC he sent his general Nearchos with three ships to explore the northern shores of the Gulf from end to end, and drew up plans for a similar expedition to explore the southern shores. This expedition never took place, due to Alexander's untimely death.

Alexander founded a trading city called Charax at the head of the Gulf, on the Shatt Al Arab. For several centuries this city was to be the great market to which ships came from the southern Gulf, from the incense lands of Yemen, from India and even from China. Pearls, purple dye (made from the murex shell), dates and gold were exported from Charax, in return for cinnamon, frankincense, copper, hard woods from India and silks from China.

Greek trade and settlements spread further down the Gulf as well. On the island of Failaka — off Kuwait, a key site in ancient times, a substantial settlement was built in Greek times too. Bahrain, whose ancient name of Dilmun was by now forgotten but whose pre-eminence on Gulf trade routes survived, was by now called Tylos or Tyros. The Greeks built a large fort there, on the site of the ancient Dilmun city on the north coast.

Greek trade came down the Gulf as far as what is now the UAE, and Greek goods were carried inland to Mleiha (near Dhaid), then a flourishing town on the caravan route to the incense lands of south Yemen. Excavations there have revealed impressive tower tombs made of mud brick in whose ruins lay pieces of broken Greek amphorae, the huge pottery vessels in which Greek goods were carried and stored. On the handles of these jars is a stamp mark in Greek giving the maker's name and the place of manufacture: the island of Rhodes.

The Greeks were interested in everything they came across in these distant lands. They left descriptions of pearl diving and of exotic plants. They were intrigued by the mangrove trees which grew in all the creeks and inlets along the coast: "Along the whole coast...grow trees resembling the laurel and the olive. When the tide ebbs the whole trees are visible above the water, and at full tide they are sometimes completely covered. This is the more singular because the coast inland has no trees." Today mangrove trees have disappeared from most of the coastline, though terebralia shells (a shellfish which lives only among the mangroves) on ancient habitation sites, show they must once have grown there. Only in Khor Kalba and around the islands of Umm Al Quwain can large mangroves be seen on UAE coasts, while small ones still grow in the creeks of Abu Dhabi and Ras Al Khaimah.

Boats of the time

Although wrecks of Greek and Roman boats have been found in the Mediterranean, no such wrecks have yet been found beneath the waters of the Gulf. However, Strabo, a Greek geographer, did take the trouble to give the following description of indigenous boats there 2,000 years ago, a description not far different from the clues left to the boats of ancient times. The mouth of the Euphrates, he wrote, "forms lakes and marshes and reed beds, which last supply reeds from which all kinds of reed-vessels are woven. Some of these vessels, when smeared all over with asphalt, can hold water, whereas the others are used in their bare state. They also make reed sails, which are similar to rush mats or wicker work."

No such boats of the period have survived to the present day, of course, but their anchors have. They used stone anchors, of roughly triangular shape with a hole bored through them for the rope. Such anchors continued in use in the Gulf until very recent times, though in later versions an iron grapnel hook was also fixed in the stone.

On the coast of the UAE near Umm Al Quwain lie the remains of a large town, Ad Dour, which flourished in the 1st century AD and continued in use to the 4th century. Several stone anchors have been found lying among its ruins. An intact small anchor had been reused as a building stone in the walls of a square fort there; another, whose lower half had broken away, was reused as the pulley to a deep well.

Large mangroves flourish at Khor Kalba.

A Greek vase found at Bidiya.
(Courtesy Fujairah Museum)

A gaming stone on the sands of Samhuram.

The Greeks themselves were intrepid seafarers and quick to exploit techniques developed by others. For centuries they were only able to follow the coastline on the voyage to India and the east, a long and tedious journey. They suspected that the local people took a more direct route across the sea, which they were not willing to divulge. A former Roman slave found the route by chance in 45 AD; he was blown out to sea in an open boat from the mouth of the Red Sea and it was only after six months that he managed to make his way back again.

A few years later a Greek pilot, Hippalus, finally worked out the secret of the monsoon winds, taking a boat directly across from the shores of Arabia to India. His discovery is described thus in a contemporary account: "This whole voyage, as above described, from Cana and Endaemon Arabia (Aden) they used to make in small vessels, sailing along around the shores of the Gulfs; and Hippalus was the pilot who by observing the location of the ports and the condition of the sea, first discovered how to lay his course straight across the ocean." It must have been a discovery at the time as momentous as the journey of Christopher Columbus to America, 1,450 years later.

This account comes from an extraordinarily early sailing manual, *The Periplus of the Erythraean Sea*, written in the 1st century AD by a Greek living in Egypt. His name is not known but he seems to have sailed the Red Sea and Indian Ocean himself, although his knowledge of the Gulf came at second hand, for the Persians were hostile to westerners at the time and kept their ships out of the Gulf.

The Periplus gives this account of maritime trade in the Gulf, 2,000 years ago: "There follows, not far beyond, the mouth of the Persian Gulf, where there is much diving for the pearl mussel...beyond which that very great and broad sea, the Persian Gulf, reaches far into the interior." In the Gulf, it records, there was a market town called Apologus, near Charax and the Euphrates River; and somewhere near the mouth of the Gulf, was another market town called Ommana, whose position is not quite clear. To both of these towns came large vessels from Barygaza (present-day Broach in India), "loaded with copper and sandalwood and timbers of teakwood and logs of blackwood and ebony. To Ommana frankincense is also brought from Cana (in south Yemen), and from Ommana to Arabia boats sewed together after the fashion of the place. From each of these market towns there are exported to Barygaza and also to Arabia many pearls."

A bronze ram's head from a Roman bowl, found at Ad Dour by Belgian archaeologists.

Arab sailors were very active in these waters by the time of *The Periplus*, whose author writes of the port of Musa (perhaps present-day Mocha in Yemen): "and the whole place is crowded with Arab shipowners and seafaring men, and is busy with the affairs of commerce; for they carry on a trade with the far side (Eritrea and Somalia) and with Barygaza, sending their own ships there."

A port of Roman times

The ancient town of Ad Dour, lying on the coast of a shallow lagoon near Umm Al Quwain, has proved of great interest to archaeologists for the site has never been inhabited again since Roman times. The pottery, glass, coins, stone anchors, fishing net weights and other objects dropped on the surface of the sand by its inhabitants in those days have been left where they fell, until today.

The large shallow lagoon on which Ad Dour stands is tidal and may have been deeper, deep enough for shallow draft boats to come in close to the town, in the heyday of the port. It was also a source of shellfish, a popular dish of the day.

The houses of the place were built of seastone, a porous stone which could be easily cut to shape. The better houses contained numerous rooms and the most impressive ones, from the later period at the beginning of the 4th century AD, were very large with round towers at the corners. A big house of this kind has been excavated on top of the sand dunes running along the shore. It had an impressive entranceway, on either side of which stood a pair of stone eagles. Within the house was found the grave of its owner, close to the grave of his camel; the sword with which the camel had been killed lay by its side.

Most impressive of the buildings found at Ad Dour was a small, finely made temple, excavated from a sand dune which had preserved the walls up to a height of two metres. The building was made of seastone but its outer walls were carefully plastered with white plaster sculpted to look like finely cut stonework. There was even an adjustment in the plaster pattern to allow for the fact that the building was constructed on slightly sloping sand.

Inside the temple a small bronze oil lamp was found, and the sculpted bronze bases of two little statues. All appear to have been imports from Rome. Outside the temple were four stone incense alters and some incense burners, indicating trade from south-eastern Arabia. One of the major trade goods of those days was frankincense, the resin of trees grown in Dhofar in southern Oman. It was exported from the picturesque port of Samhuram, near present-day Salalah.

Of particular interest at Ad Dour were the large numbers of very well-made, stone-lined tombs discovered all over the site. Some of these tombs still had intact stone vaulted or corbelled roofs. Objects from the tombs included fine bronze drinking sets of Mediterranean style, and many beautiful glass flasks of Roman design, which must have been made in Rome, Syria or Egypt. The colourful glazed pottery of the place, on the other hand, had mostly been brought from Persia to the north, while the coins, when not local, were often from northern Arabia and Charax.

Pottery from Persia and fragments of glass from Rome or Syria on the sands at Ad Dour.

A dhow sails along Dubai Creek in the 1950s.
(Photo: Neville Allen)

SONS OF SINDBAD

"Blessed with a favouring wind, we sped upon the foamy highways of the sea, trading from port to port and from island to island."

Sindbad the Sailor

Although Arabs are more generally thought of as desert dwellers, masters of the great camel caravan routes across the empty wastes, in fact the long coastlines of Arabia led many to take to the seas instead. All along the Arab shores there was an ancient tradition of seafaring, and coastal peoples were more at home on the waters than in the sands. From times long ago, the Gulf had been more of a highway than a hindrance.

In the early days of the great Islamic expansion, however, the vast majority of tribes from inner Arabia had no dealings with the coast apart from trade at market towns, and they found it difficult to come to terms with this facility for life at sea. When the Arab leader Mu'awiya asked permission to embark his men on ships, the Caliph Omar consulted his general, Amr who replied: "The sea is a boundless expanse whereon great ships look like tiny specks; nought but the heavens above and waters beneath; when calm the sailor's heart is broken; when tempestuous his senses reel. Trust it little, fear it much. Man at sea is an insect on a splinter, now engulfed, now scared to death." So the Caliph refused permission, saying, "The safety of my people is dearer to me than all the treasures of Greece." Within a few years, however, Mu'awiya's fleet seized Cyprus, and by 655 AD the Arabs were able to defeat the Byzantine emperor in a big naval battle in the eastern Mediterranean.

When the Abbasids established the capital of the Islamic empire in Baghdad in the 8th century, it gave a great boost to shipping in the Gulf, one of the main trade routes for provisions to the capital.

19

Strips of pure cotton are sewn together for sails.

Preparing to hoist the sail of a dhow.

Arab sailors had already explored the distant seas, far beyond the Strait of Hormuz.

Early Arab seafaring

Arab sailors from the Gulf region made their way to India long before the Romans discovered the secret of the monsoon winds. It was, indeed, the attractive nature of the trade goods which they brought back from there, and especially the spices of the east, that encouraged the Romans to launch out onto the Indian Ocean.

The secret of this Arab seafaring success is thought to have been the development of the lateen sail, a specially set sail which was in universal use in the region until very recent times and which may still occasionally be seen on big dhows today. In the earliest times boats were sailed with a square sail, set at right angles to the wind. With a following wind this worked very well, but in any other wind it was of little use. Sailors soon realised that long journeys could only be made if boats could sail with the wind from the side, or even partly from in front.

Sometime around the beginning of this era, Arabs sailing in the Gulf and the Indian Ocean found that their sails would work better if set along the line of the boat, and better still when tilted down at the front. So they developed the lateen sail, a sail which is much shorter at the front edge than the back, and which hangs from a long spar slung obliquely from high on the mast. This lateen could sail far closer to the wind than any sail designed before. It was made of strips of cotton cloth, or of reed or palm-frond matting.

The Arab ships of those early times may not have been so far removed from ships in use right up to the present day. Initially, however, their steering was less efficient. They depended on a side rudder, a large oar hung out on either side towards the back of the boat. By the 13th century AD, they developed a rudder fixed to the stern, but controlled at first by ropes to either side. Such rudders survived into the 20th century on small fishing boats called 'badans', along the coasts of Oman and the UAE.

The planks of the hull in early Arab ships were sewn together with stitching of coconut fibre, a method which continued into the 16th and 17th centuries, and occasionally found in the 20th century. It was described in the 12th century by the Arab geographer, Ibn Jubayr: "They are stitched with cords of coir which is the coconut; this they thrash until it becomes stringy, then they twist from it cords with which they stitch the ships."

***The Sohar, a completely traditional boum with
sewn planks, voyaged to China.***

The earliest known picture of an Arab sea-going
trading vessel is from the Maqamat of Al Hariri, a
book made in Iraq in 1237 AD. It shows a ship
which is just like a boum (one of the most familiar
dhows in the Gulf today). The ship in the picture
has a long, upward-pointing bowsprit, a stern
rudder, sewn planks, and a line of little merchants'
faces looking wanly out of portholes along the side.

The boum is still the primary trading ship of the
Gulf. It has kept to the traditional local design of
a pointed stern, unlike most of the other boats in
the Gulf. It can be made in very large sizes, up to
65 metres in length, and its most characteristic
feature is the high, straight bow, set at an angle of
45 degrees. This bowsprit has intrigued marine
experts who have suggested that it is a relic of more
ancient times, when ships had square sails set at
right angles to the hull. Such sails would have
needed a foreward stay to tie them down at the
front, and the boum's bowsprit may have been the
place to which they were tied.

The seaworthiness of a boum with sewn planks
was proved in 1980 by the adventurous traveller,
Tim Severin. He built a completely traditional boum,
named 'The Sohar', in the shipyards at Sur in Oman,
and sailed it on a 9,000-kilometre journey across
the oceans to China. His boat has now been brought
back to Oman and is on display on a roundabout
in the Al Bustan Bay.

Navigation

Seafarers of the Gulf became experts in the science of navigation from a very early period. The 8th-century Abbasid empire, with its centre at Baghdad, encouraged scholars to study the sciences of all kinds. They made particularly important progress in astronomy; Muslim astronomers of the period were able to carry the science far further than the Greeks had ever done. Sailors in the Gulf, so close to Baghdad, must have been the first to benefit from these researches.

They were experts at tracking their routes from the stars. They used a finger's width measurement which they called 'isba'; 224 isba was equal to 360 degrees. Another measuring device was the 'kamal', a small oblong of wood through which was passed a knotted cord. By measuring the height of the Pole Star above the horizon the sailors were able to make an accurate calculation of latitude.

Arab navigators were also intensely pragmatic in collecting and recording their seafaring knowledge. They developed marine manuals incorporating the discoveries of generations of sailors, of which the earliest surviving one dates from the 10th century, by Al Muqaddasi. He describes a sea voyage he made with experienced sailors: "I have seen in their possession sailing directories which they constantly study and follow with implicit confidence."

One of the most famous compilers of these manuals was Ahmad ibn Majid, an experienced Arab navigator of the 15th century. He was the son and grandson of professional navigators and collected together the works of his father and grandfather, as well as his own. In all, he compiled some 40 manuals of seafaring, incorporating works of the early 10th century as well as those of his own family.

Ibn Majid is of particular interest to the lower Gulf since he is believed to have been born at Julfar, near Ras Al Khaimah, and lived part of his life in Muscat. His manuals describe these seas and coasts, as well as the Red Sea and Indian Ocean. In one of the manuals, written in verse and dated to about 1490, he gives an account of the journey from the Tunbs islands, off the coast of Ras Al Khaimah, to Sharjah, then north along the coast to Umm Al Quwain and Ras Al Khaimah.

Most important of all for them, perhaps, was an accurate knowledge of the currents and winds in the seas in which they sailed. For the journey to the east, the most vital winds were the monsoons: the south-west monsoon would carry a sailing ship to India, and the north-east monsoon (which blows from October to March), would bring it back. The north-east monsoon would also take a sailing ship down the east coast of Africa, a trip which could be made in as little as three weeks in February and March when there was a following current.

Lateen sails carried Arab seafarers to India, China and Africa.

Distant journeys

By the 8th century sailors of the Gulf were travelling very far indeed, as far in fact as China. The Abbasid capital at Baghdad, one of the greatest cities in the world at the time, provided an eager market for exotic luxury goods of all kinds. At the other end of the trade route, the great Tang dynasty was a powerful contemporary. Gulf ships came back regularly from the Far East laden with silks, camphor, musk and spices. In exchange they carried out cargoes of linen, cotton, woollen cloths, rugs, metalwork, iron ore and bullion. Their journeys were described by a number of famous Arab geographers in the 9th and 10th centuries. Indeed, their real exploits provided the raw material for the collection of stories of Sindbad the Sailor.

At that time Arabs and Persians sailed together. The language of seafaring was Arabic but many Persian words concerning the sea crept into it, such as bandar (port), nakhuda (captain), and sambuq (a kind of dhow). The population of many of the ports on both sides of the Gulf was mixed Arab and Persian by descent.

The Musandam forms a mountainous backdrop.

In the records of the Tang dynasty is the complaint that in the year 758 AD "the Tah-shih (Arabs) and Po-sse (Persians) together sacked and burned the city of Kwang-chon (Canton) and then sailed back to sea." In those days it was a four-month journey from the Gulf to Canton; the round trip, determined by the monsoons, took a year and a quarter to complete.

Meanwhile sailors from the Gulf continued to ply the routes to India, bringing from the major ports there teak for their boats, rice, spices and other foods. From about 700 AD onwards they were also sailing southwards, along the east coast of Africa. In the 10th century the Arab writer, Al Masudi, commented of those sea lanes: "The people who sail on this sea are Omani Arabs of the tribe of Azd." The Omani settlers established colonies at Mogadishu, Lamu, Mombasa and several island settlements off the coast of Africa. It was the start of a coastal empire which was to bring huge wealth to Oman, especially in the 19th century, when cloves from Zanzibar were a great cash crop.

A thousand years earlier, in the 9th century, the port of Sohar on the Omani coast far surpassed any other port in the region as a hub of trade. At first sight, Sohar does not seem a likely place for a great international maritime emporium. There is no natural harbour there, simply an open anchorage on a low-lying coast. But the great Wadi Jizzi which runs inland just to the north of Sohar provided the main overland trade route through to the Gulf coast and the important Gulf port of Julfar (near Ras Al Khaimah). Its waters nourished the greatest agricultural development in the Oman peninsula on the plain around Sohar, ensuring adequate supplies of fresh fruit and vegetables, along with quantities of dried fish and limes, for ships starting out on long voyages.

At its height, in the 10th century, Sohar was described by contemporary writers as "the emporium of the whole world". In 917 the governor of Sohar sent presents to the Caliph in Baghdad, whose help he was soliciting. He selected a range of exotic creatures: a talking mynah bird from India, monkeys from Indonesia, a giant ant from Africa, and a number of huge serpents and other wonders of the oceans. From Africa, Sohar brought ivory, gold, tortoise shell, leopard skins and ambergris, commodities in demand at home and favoured for export to China. From China they brought back silks, camphor, musk and spices and from India teak and more spices.

This far-flung international trade could bring great profit. A later study of the medieval pepper trade told that pepper was purchased for two grams of silver per kilogram in the Indies, sold for 10 to 14g in Alexandria, 14 to 18g in Venice and by the time it reached the consumers in northern Europe the price was 20 to 30g of silver per kg.

Sohar was at the heart of such trade in its heyday. The 10th century geographer, Al Muqaddasi, wrote an even more glowing account of the results of such trade: "No more distinguished city exists today in the China Sea: it is prosperous, populous, exquisite, pleasant and honourable....a refined city stretching along the coast. Its inhabitants have houses of brick and teak wood...and enjoy an abundance of all things. It is the hallway to China, the store house of the East and Iraq and the stay of the Yemen." But disaster struck before his ink was dry on the paper: Sohar was sacked twice in quick succession in 965 and again in 971 AD. The kilns used for firing

The fort of Sohar stands on the tell of what was the greatest emporium of medieval times.

Spices of the East were the prize for long voyages.

the building bricks, along with much of the town, were abandoned after such terrible devastation. But the bricks made in them continued to be used and reused until the present day, worn down now to half their original size.

For the short period of a century or so, Sohar had dominated the greatest trade route of the medieval world. Not surprisingly it was to become the reputed home of the legendary Sindbad the Sailor. Today a sprawling mound, or tell, by the seashore marks the heart of the prosperous medieval port; a white-painted fort at the top stands on the site of much older, brick-built forts of Sohar's prime.

Throughout these centuries there was a rival to Sohar on the opposite side of the Oman peninsula. This was the port of Julfar on the Gulf coast of what is now the UAE. Julfar flourished from the 7th century AD, becoming an important port recorded by geographers and historians throughout the centuries, and finally and fatally attracting the attention of the Portuguese for its wealth in the early 17th century.

Recent excavations beside the sea to the north of Ras Al Khaimah have revealed the streets and houses, fort and mosque of the town which flourished there from the 14th to 17th centuries. Of the earlier Julfar there is as yet no trace. But the Julfar which the archaeologists have uncovered accords well with the ancient records: it was a place of great trade, especially with China and the Far East. Great quantities of broken pieces of fine Chinese porcelain have been found on the site, and it is indeed these which have provided so certain a dating for the place.

Most famous of all trading centres in the Gulf region, however, was undoubtedly Hormuz. This island city, strategically placed at the entrance to the Strait which bears its name, was to become by the 15th century an independent kingdom. The town had originally been founded on the mainland, north of the Gulf, near present-day Bandar Abbas. In the 13th century it was ruled by an Arab dynasty, but after Tartar raids in the region the inhabitants moved across to the island of Hormuz for greater security. By 1400 Hormuz was master of the lower Gulf, controlling Ras Al Khaimah, Julfar and Bahrain.

But stories of its wealth had travelled far and wide. When the Portuguese sailed into the Gulf in 1507, Hormuz was to be their principal goal, their greatest prize.

A lateen sail fills in the wind.

aloes wood, sandalwood, saffron, indigo, wax, iron, sugar, rice, coconut, precious stones and porcelain "from all of which they make a great deal of money," he wrote.

The Portuguese, too, were to make a great deal of money from Hormuz. Their customs receipts from the island brought in more than the combined trade of their two main Eastern ports, Goa and Malacca. But their customs officials were not immune to temptation. In 1550 officials were sent from Goa to monitor the receipts of Hormuz; customs revenues more than doubled during their stay.

Control of Hormuz and the export trade of the Gulf was not enough for the Portuguese, who were tempted by stories of the great pearl fisheries of Bahrain, to send a ship across to those islands. Their sailors landed and walked inland until they came to a large mosque. Seeing no one they discreetly returned to their ships. Conquest looked simple and soon after, in 1522, they returned, attacked the town and killed the Ruler of the island.

Bahrain was not so easy to hold, however, and the Portuguese had to beat off rebellion from within and attack from without. In 1560, after a Turkish attack, they set about remodelling the old fort on the north coast, incorporating all the most up-to-date features of European military architecture, and making it one of the strongest forts in the Gulf.

They held Bahrain until 1602, when the great fort was lost through negligence rather than superior force. Hormuz they finally lost 20 years later, to a combined attack by Persians and British, a new power in the region. And so they moved to Julfar. In 1621 a Portuguese captain had set up his cannons in a mosque to bombard the fort there. In 1631 the Portuguese built a fort of their own in Julfar but their hold of it was to be short-lived for local forces seized Julfar from them in 1633.

Chinese porcelain

During Portuguese control in the Gulf, trade with China reached its zenith. This trade had been started by Arab sailors many centuries earlier, and for several hundred years the Arabs of the Gulf had been importing the very high quality porcelain in which Chinese manufacturers specialised. In the 16th century these imports soared, for they were greatly in demand by the Portuguese. The earliest Chinese porcelain to reach the Gulf came in the 14th century. There was the olive-green celadon ware whose colour came from iron in the glaze, and of which mostly bowls and deep dishes were imported.

Square sterns followed Portuguese influence. (Photo: Neville Allen)

Bahrain's fort was greatly strengthened by the Portuguese.

The most popular porcelain, however, was the Chinese blue-and-white, a very fine porcelain, produced for many centuries, and at its best during the Ming dynasty, from the mid-14th to mid-17th centuries.

Fragments of blue-and-white porcelain can be found on settlement sites near the coast in Bahrain, the UAE and Oman. They are an important key for archaeologists for these bowls and dishes were marked on the base with the date and name of the ruling Chinese emperor, and thus provide a clue to the date of the Arab settlement in which they are found.

The blue colour for the designs was made from cobalt, of which only a poor-quality kind was found in China. The best cobalt was exported from Persia for use in China. In later times the Persians themselves made copies of Chinese blue-and-white ware; they achieved a fine blue colour but a poor quality porcelain.

Detail of a Chinese porcelain dish in RAK Museum.

British in the Gulf

In the 17th century the British, following the Portuguese, were extending their trade with India and the Far East. For the British, India was to become their most important overseas territory, the jewel in the crown of their expanding empire.

The Gulf provided the shortest route to India (via the Mediterranean and Iraq) so control of Gulf trade routes became of increasing importance to British shipping. They set up trading factories on the Persian side of the Gulf and until the mid-18th century their trade flowed freely, for the Gulf was dominated by the Shah of Persia. Persian power declined after the mid-century, however, and towards the end of the century the British came into conflict with the rising Arab maritime power of the Qawasim. The Qawasim controlled both shores of the lower Gulf from their bases at Ras Al Khaimah and Sharjah on the southern coast, and Qishm and Lingeh on the Persian coast. The British accused them of attacks on their shipping and in 1809 attacked Ras Al Khaimah in retribution.

The Arab ships were faster than those of the British, sailing close to the wind with their lateen sails. They were also of shallower draft, which enabled them to take shelter from their pursuers, hiding out in the creeks and inlets along the coasts of the mountainous Musandam Peninsula and the shallow sandy shores that are now in the UAE. Behind each town on that coast was a hidden creek, offering a perfect refuge for the Arab dhows but unapproachable by the deeper-draft British craft.

For a few years after the attack on Ras Al Khaimah there was peace in the Gulf, but it didn't last and in 1819 the British decided to enforce maritime peace definitively. That same year they attacked Ras Al Khaimah again, and followed the retreating Qawasim to the near-impregnable fort on a peak at Dhayah. They dragged their cannon five kilometres inland from the sea and bombarded the fort, which eventually surrendered. The British took or destroyed the Qawasim ships and demolished the defences of Ras Al Khaimah. In January 1820 they called all the sheikhs of the coastal towns to Falayah Fort, near Ras Al Khaimah, to sign a General Treaty of Peace which would guarantee the peace at sea.

The Maritime Peace Treaty had the advantage for the British that their ships could trade and transit in the Gulf without let or hindrance. It also ensured the safety of the Arabs' own trading vessels and of the vital pearling fleets which had until then been subject to sporadic attacks on the pearling banks in the summer. By the early 20th century, great merchant pearling dynasties were established along the whole length of the Gulf.

The great tower of Ras Al Khaimah fort.

Above and below: Dhow builders work with traditional tools as they chip and saw the teak to shape the keel.

The methods and tools of the boat-builders have changed remarkably little over the centuries. In the dhow yards today one can observe a craft which is hundreds, probably thousands, of years old, still practised in much the same way as it ever was. The carpenters work with remarkable speed and accuracy with simple tools: chisel, adze and hammer, saw and plane.

In the last few decades they have lightened the load by the addition of band saws, electric drills, and small electric chain saws. But for the most part, they are at work with their old tools, slicing off the thinnest slivers of wood, and fitting plank to plank with precision.

In English all these wooden boats are collectively referred to as dhows, but this is not a name used by their Arab owners who call them by their individual names, or nowadays 'lanchaat' for those which are driven by motor.

Construction methods

When a dhow is ordered, and the down-payment received, the builders simply go straight to work. There are no drawings or plans, though a prospective owner may roughly sketch out his ideas with a piece of chalk on a plank. The methods are well-tried and the master builders have a true eye.

First the keel is laid. This consists of a long and heavy teak beam laid on small blocks of wood on the sand. In the past, the laying of the keel was the most anxious time in the construction of the dhow, and new keels were often protected by a fence. For there was a strong belief that if a woman who had borne no children could jump across the newly laid keel of a dhow she would conceive a baby. But, it was also thought, the jinns watching over the dhows would inevitably take a life for a life: either the nakhuda would be lost at sea or one of the carpenters was soon to die. So the carpenters worked in the past with desperate speed to lay enough planks that no female could jump them.

Today there is no sign of this superstition; the planks are slotted carefully and at leisure into grooves along the keel, and in the stem and stern posts which are bolted to the keel from the start. These first planks are not easy to fit, since they must have a pronounced twist to give the shape of the boat, and much tapping and hammering is required to get them just right. They are then nailed down, and held in place by little blocks of wood fixed temporarily on the outside to hold the shape.

The dhow yards along the creekside in Ajman are the largest in the Gulf.

Thus the ship is built up little by little, and only as it grows are the ribs, made of crooked lengths of wood, put into place inside it. Eventually all the planks will be nailed down to the ribs, the nail holes running in neat rows up and down the sides of the ship. These holes are now drilled out with an electric drill. In the past the work was far more arduous as a bow drill was used. Today the hole is quickly made, wider at the outside so the large head of the nail may be countersunk. Once the nail is in place, the hole is stopped with mastic.

The planks, which abut neatly (unlike European boats where the planks often overlap), must be sealed. This is done by pushing a soft string into all the joints, then the whole boat is oiled with fish oil to keep it waterproof. By now it may be a very tall ship, balanced precariously on its keel, with upright props nailed to the sides as the boat grows.

Once the woodwork is complete the finishing touches can be added. Today a motor is always installed, a propeller is fitted just above the end of the keel, a deck for fishing boats and a little cabin for traders. Decoration is popular, especially for the

A carpenter fits the first planks to the keel.

Checking the nail holes on a dhow about to be launched.

Large dhows, of the kind built in the Hamriya yard in Dubai, are a much bigger investment. This yard builds boats of a 100 tonnes and up, the only place in the Gulf to do so, and its customers come from all the neighbouring states. These boats are strongly built, expected to last 45 to 50 years, but take 10 to 12 months to complete. One large dhow under construction was a massive boat, 35 metres long, destined by its Kuwaiti owner to become a floating hotel. It is estimated that the very large dhows cost some Dh2 million to build, giving a total of around Dh3 million when the engine and other fittings are installed.

Once clear of its supporting tyres, the dhow lurches alarmingly as a bulldozer pushes it into the water.

New departures

Dhow-building in the Gulf has, since time immemorial, depended on the import of wood from India. The preferred wood here is teak, a wood so valuable that European boat yards can scarcely afford to use it for their decks alone. Teak does not shrink, split, crack or distort. It is extremely durable, easily worked, and is not affected by the iron nails holding it in place. It was imported by all the ancient civilisations of the Gulf region; a comment of about 300 BC shows the Greeks' admiration for this wood: "In the Island of Tylus (Bahrain) off the Arabian coast they say that there is a kind of wood of which they build their ships, and that in seawater this is almost proof against decay; for it lasts more than 20 years if it is kept under water."

In the Gulf today the boat will be built of teak, but with mangrove poles and 'jungle wood' crooks for the ribs. In recent times wood has been growing scarcer in India. The dhow yard in Ras Al Khaimah complained of long waits for the next load.

In the early 1990s, however, dhow yards branched out into new technology, following the lead of the small fishing boats which are now almost universally made of fibreglass. Fibreglass dhows, of the same size and same style as the wooden ones, appeared in the yards of Ajman, and in some specialist fibreglass factories in Sharjah as well.

These dhows are made up, layer by layer, inside a wooden mould which looks somewhat like a flimsy dhow. Several dhows can be made successively in the same mould. The fishermen say these dhows ride higher in the water, since unlike the wooden dhows, they do not become saturated. They require less maintenance and are expected to last longer. That is, provided nothing goes wrong. Once a fibreglass dhow has an accident it is more complicated to mend and requires lifting gear to take it out of the water. Such facilities are available in Dubai Creek but not in Kuwait, whose owners still therefore order wooden dhows.

Fibreglass dhows lack the beauty of wooden ones, for all that they are built to the same design. But their day seems to be dawning: by early 1992, six of the 42 dhows under construction in Ajman were made of fibreglass.

Finishing touches to the deck of a fibreglass dhow.

Wooden mould for a fibreglass dhow.

spotted. This boat then lays a seine net around the shoal, its ends coming into the beach.

A team of half-a-dozen men takes each end of the net, pulling it gradually into shore in unison. The task is a long and heavy one, the men chanting as they haul on the net for a couple of hours or so. They are directed by a man standing in the little fishing boat and waving a cloth to indicate which side should pull. As the net comes in close to the shore all look anxiously at the water within its crescent. If the water begins to boil, and seagulls come swooping low over it, then they know that all is well; they have taken a good catch. But sometimes at the end of hours of work there will be nothing; the shoal has slipped out of the trap.

If the catch is good it will be collected in large bags and tipped immediately into a pick-up truck on the beach. Many fishermen reckon that the catch from these seine nets represents over a third of their annual haul from the sea.

For work close to the shore the fishermen use a number of small boats, some of very ancient design. Little dug-out canoes, known as houris, were once common along the coasts. They could be easily paddled out to waiting boats or traps, and could be made deeper by the addition of a few planks above the dug-out keel. Today only a few are still in use, but others can be seen from time to time, abandoned on the shore.

An even more primeval boat, the shasha, is still used along the east coast of the UAE and the Batinah of Oman, though its days too are probably numbered. As described in chapter one, the shasha has been adapted to modern life, and the stern modified to take an outboard motor. Early in 1992 I counted 13 of them on the beach between Fujairah and Khor Kalba, of which only two were no longer in use. There were a further four on the beach of Qurayyah, seemingly little used. Three were in good working condition on the beach of Bidiya: one was

Today's shashas are modified and given a double stern to take an outboard motor.

Badans could not be adapted to a motor so must still be rowed.

three years old, another two years and the third made during the previous year.

Most of the Gulf's fishermen now go to sea in business-like fibreglass boats with a couple of outboard motors at the back. Their old wooden boats lie abandoned around the little harbours. Only occasionally now may one see an old badan, the elegant high-sterned 'sardine boat' which was once so prevalent in Oman and on the east coast of the UAE. These boats were of venerable lineage: the rudder was attached to the high vertical stern and manipulated with ropes, as in ancient times. However, an outboard motor cannot be fitted to the pointed stern, so the badan has lost its importance in the fishing fleets of the coast.

The modern fishing boats cluster for preference in a creek or small harbour; when neither is available they must be left at anchor offshore, or pulled laboriously up onto the beach. Palm-frond shelters often line the fishing beaches, where the fishermen sit in the afternoons, mending the nets and adjusting the floats and sinkers.

In the evening they will set off for the fishing grounds, each boat carrying a little light to mark its position. The nets will be lowered into the water, the fish traps pulled up on board, emptied, then set back in the sea. By the morning the small boats

will be coming back into their home harbour, hopefully loaded with the fruits of the sea.

Slightly bigger boats also make their way out to the fishing grounds, especially at the weekends. These boats have long rods protruding above their cabins; they are the boats of the sport fishermen who go out to take large game fish by rod and line. The waters of the Gulf offer some exciting fishing of this kind — sailfish, barracuda and king mackerel for example — and the fishermen have the satisfaction of providing their families with an excellent feast at the end of the day.

Largest of the fishing boats are the shu'ais, which go far out onto the ocean and stay away for several days. The large boats have a covered deck, below which the fish are stored in containers with ice. When such a boat comes into shore its hold may be filled with many baskets, each arranged to contain fish of a given kind.

Some of these fishing dhows specialise in catching sharks. They come back to land with a clutch of these 'monsters of the deep' and perhaps a collection of little ones as well. So heavy are the sharks that such boats need a lifting winch to pull their catch up from the hold. One such boat, fishing off Kalba on the east coast of the UAE in 1991, came back with a five-metre-long shark weighing

No time is wasted — fresh fish are quickly unloaded at the end of the trip.

700 kilograms, taken just four kilometres offshore.

Occasionally the fishermen take a poor small whale, the whale shark, in their nets. These harmless creatures are mistaken for dangerous sharks, because of their size, and are usually left to die on the shore.

A fish industry

The most noticeable of the fish industries in the Gulf is also undoubtedly the most ancient one. This is the process of drying the shoals of small fish taken in the seine nets. These fish are simply spread out on the sand and left for several days to dry in the sun. At the end of that time they are scraped together, piled into bags and taken off to the market. They are used mostly for animal fodder, and also for fertiliser, and they may be exported. A few dried fish are still bought in the souq as an edible delicacy; they are usually eaten crumbled over a bed of rice.

Larger fish may also be dried, especially sharks' fins which are mostly dried for export. And sometimes they are packed in salt into big tins, also for export.

In recent years the Gulf states have been looking into the possibilities of more-modern fish processing. Factories have been set up to freeze prawns and other fish, especially for the export market. Saudi Fisheries is the largest commercial fishing company in the Gulf. Each year their 25 shrimp trawlers take some 3,000 tonnes of shrimp which normally proliferate in the warm Gulf waters, from their breeding grounds in the Tigris-Euphrates delta. They were badly affected, however, by oil slicks following the Gulf War and 90 per cent of the shrimps in the upper Gulf were reported lost. Other fishing in these waters was reduced too.

Nets are cleaned and hung to dry after each fishing trip.

compartments or boxes might be cunningly concealed behind two of the bottom drawers of the chest; these were shortened to accommodate the box, which was attached to the central divider between them. Lids were secured by two or three long hinges with decorative heads. Side handles, either fixed to a plate or directly into the chest, made it easier to carry. Most chests were locked with a padlock through a clasp and staple. They had strips of flat beading round the top of the lid, corners and side edges. Brasswork, never copper, in the form of plaques, sheets or studs, embellished the chest in accordance with local custom. Studs were handmade with domed heads and square shafts, often totally of brass, though the very large studs could be solid and fixed with iron pins. Drawers, edged with narrow flat beading, might have one or two handles, and brasswork and studs to match the decoration of the chest.

Smaller chests of similar proportions up to two feet (0.61 metre) in length were also numerous. These were either plain, carved or decorated with brass studs and/or plating. Inside, a framework of compartments, some lidded, hinged or inset, supports a central oblong tray, divided into two parts lengthwise. Depending on the sophistication of the chest, secret compartments of great complexity may be found beneath this framework. Carving or inlaid brass wire frequently embellishes the interior. A plain exterior often conceals the delicate and intricate decoration within, consisting of carving or inlaid brass wire. The lid, if it fits flush with the body of the box, is deep and fitted internally with several narrow horizontal strips of wood for holding papers and stationery. An overlapping lid had no room for these, however, such chests were made in India after the western manner in the 19th century onwards, and were intended to be writing boxes. They lock with a key and are still used by traders as cash boxes.

Sea chests are an essential in maritime countries, each sailor possessing his own, and the captain probably more than one. They were not ornate, as much brasswork would not be practical at sea. Some were even bound overall with rope for ease of handling; these were longer than average for their width and height, and came from Calicut on the Malabar coast of India. Very small boxes were also used for pearls, which were stored in bags in the various compartments.

A fine Arab chest, probably made in the Gulf over 50 years ago, adorns a modern living room.

Trade in chests

A colourful chest from the Sharqiya area of Oman. (Photo: Sheila Unwin)

Chests are found in all countries of the Gulf and Arabia, Iraq and Yemen, across the Red Sea to Somalia, Kenya, Tanzania, Zanzibar and beyond. In fact, wherever the Arab traded or settled, his chest went with him — his suitcase for the journey and his storage box on arrival. When the popularity of chests in the Gulf had passed, many were cast aside. This was quickly noted by the astute dhow captains who habitually voyaged to East Africa via the annual dhow trade, sailing from the Gulf on the north-east monsoon from October to March, and returning on the south-west monsoon from April to September. Even when motorised the dhows kept to this pattern. The main purpose of these voyages was to collect mangrove poles used in the building industry in the Gulf, which were to be found on the Rufiji Delta, Tanzania, and at Lamu in Kenya. The chests, which were picked up from Gulf ports and Oman in the off-season, were a welcome ballast cargo. On arrival at port, they were sold to a trader or an individual in customs houses in Zanzibar before the 1964 revolution, and in the Old Port at Mombasa thereafter.

The dhow trade to Africa ended in the late 1960s and traders in the Gulf concentrated on selling the chests locally. This was not difficult, with a large expatriate population and the renewed interest of local people in their past treasures. By the late 1980s quality chests had become rare, and Oman, where the majority of old chests were to be found, imposed a ban on export. None the less, resourceful traders found ways round this, the result being that some old chests are still available in Dubai and Sharjah, for example, but anything really good has become expensive. Clearly the supply will not last for ever, and the days when there was a choice of chests in the souks of Oman and the Gulf are rapidly diminishing; they are seldom seen nowadays on the East African coast.

What are their origins? Where were they made? It has often been assumed that because chests are termed 'Arab' they were made in Arabia. Some undoubtedly were, but in relatively modern times. Their sources lie in India, and it seems likely that the term refers to those who used the chests rather than to where they were actually made.

Origins of chests

As Arabia is a relatively unforested area, with the exception of parts of Oman and Yemen, timber was one of the main imports, which was principally sought from the Malabar coast, where in the past there were large stands of teak, rosewood, and shishum, a similar hard blackwood. The finest teak came from Burma, which was shipped or towed to entrepots such as Surat in Gujarat and Calicut for onward disposal. Other qualities were from the

65

Italy, evaporated milk, motor vehicles and TV sets. Above all, Dubai's well-connected merchants had realised that fortunes could be made by supplying their customers with goods they really wanted, and could not get easily from anywhere else. By 1970 Dubai, with a population of 80,000 at the time, was buying 20 per cent of the world's total gold production, and was the third largest buyer in the world of Swiss watches.

This did not mean that Dubai's women were walking around weighed down with gold, nor the men struggling with two or three watches on each wrist. Instead, discreet dhows slipped out of her creek, loaded with gold tola bars and watches, bound for the coasts of India where they would be just as discreetly unloaded for a market where gold fetched twice the price it did in Dubai.

By 1972 there were already more dhows in Dubai Creek than in any port other than Bombay. In November of that year the town was visited by E and C Martin, authors of *Cargoes of the East*. They counted 183 dhows moored on Deira side and 21 on Dubai side. Cargoes for Iran, already a major market accounting for some 40 per cent of Dubai's dhow trade, included radios, record players, cigarettes and clothes; from Iran the dhows brought fruit, vegetables, live animals and passengers.

Four years later another writer, David Howarth, author of *Dhows*, noted over a hundred ships in the creek while along the wharves were piles of lentils, onions, dates, limes, tomatoes, refrigerators, mattresses, wheelbarrows, WCs, washing machines, air-conditioners, freezers, tea, shoes, carpets, motorcycles, umbrellas, cars and teak wood. Dhows

Dhows wait to load, several abreast.

Prows of a boum and a shu'ai. (Photo: M Pettipher)

at this time were often serving as lighters, to unload the hundred or so big ships waiting offshore for a berth in the overworked Port Rashid.

Dhow trade today

In November 1991, exactly 19 years after the Martins visited Dubai, I again counted the dhows in the creek, anxiously wondering whether their numbers would have fallen so very much. I need not have worried. Along Deira side 194 dhows were moored (including a score of fishing dhows near the Sheraton Hotel), while on Dubai side there were 38. But that was not all. In Hamriya Port, constructed since the Martins' visit and opened in 1979, another 110 dhows were loading busily, and many of them were of the very large ocean-going kind. So there were one-and-a-half times as many dhows in Dubai at that time as there had been almost 20 years ago. Overall,

some 6,000 dhows come into the creek each year, and they can be up to 400 or 500 tonnes in weight.

Most of their cargo is loaded by hand. Those dhows aiming to take on larger loads, such as pick-up trucks and cars, tend to stop in Hamriya Port where small cranes are available. Along the quays are stacks of car tyres, iron rods and building materials, sacks of flour, tins of ghee and tomatoes, armchairs and sofas, computers, baby milk, TV sets and stereos, cookers, fridges, washing machines, wheelbarrows, toys, glasses, radios, light bulbs and silks. The cases carry exotic labels: "Made in — Taiwan, Korea, China, the USA, Shanghai, Japan, Singapore, England" — to name but a selection.

Some 800 dhows are registered as Dubai-owned. The rest belong to merchants in Iran, Pakistan or India. The methods of organising the trade are as varied as are the cargoes. An owner-merchant may carry his own goods, and those of some of his fellows (as in the early part of the century). Or the dhow may take any cargo which comes its way.

Cargo stacked on the quay awaiting loading.

Ropes and spars at the prow of a dhow.

Its success, and the speed with which it fills its hold while alongside Dubai's quays, depends on the energy and enterprise of the captain, the nakhuda. He must do the rounds of the merchants in the souq; drink endless small glasses of sweet tea with those who come along the shore, put up a hand-written sign perhaps of his destination, and try his utmost to fill his boat, while his crew manhandle the goods on deck. Some dhows which do not manage to fill in Hamriya Port move on into the creek where they are closer to the markets.

In the early 1990s dhows were sailing from Dubai to almost as wide a range of destinations as they ever did, with the exception of the east African ports down to Zanzibar, an important area of trade up to the mid-century. Today Iran is by far the major market, with some 18,000 dhows making the round trip each year. India comes next (about 800 voyages), followed by Somalia (about 350) — a trade for big dhows which is now a profitable one, especially for those carrying Somali goods on into Saudi Arabia. All the Gulf ports attract dhow traffic from Dubai, the major one being Bahrain, which itself had an active local dhow trade with Saudi Arabia before the road causeway was opened, putting the dhows out of work. The ocean-going dhows visiting Bahrain tie up in Mina Manama, just off-shore of the souq and close to the traditional old dhow harbour, now lost through land reclamation. From the Gulf a few intrepid dhows go as far afield as Singapore, Sri Lanka, Kenya, Yemen, Djibouti and Ethiopia.

It is a tribute to the solidity of these relatively small wooden craft, open to the elements, that they can undertake such long, sea-going voyages, heavily loaded as they appear to be when they leave Dubai's shores. Half-a-dozen cars may be lashed to the deck of a small dhow, or her gunwales may be raised by rows of cords to prevent a high-piled load from slipping into the ocean. How, one wonders, will they ever make it to the other side?

Yet clearly they do, just as they have always done. If it were no longer possible to observe this antique trade with one's own eyes, it would be hard to credit the tales of the times of Sindbad the sailor, the great days of Sohar's dhow trade with China, the Indian subcontinent, and the spice islands of the Far East.

Today the dhows sailing out of Dubai are engaged largely in the re-export trade. Indeed, Dubai's trade is still mostly entrepot, a trade worth three times as much as her non-oil export trade (Dh7.6 billion for entrepot as against Dh2.5 for direct exports). The dhows manage to handle 45 per cent by weight

A derrick barge leaving Dubai Creek. (Courtesy McDermott)

of the Emirate's total re-exports. Today the major items of this entrepot trade are textiles, electronic goods, electrical appliances, motor vehicles, silver bullion and car spare parts. Some 25 per cent of all re-exports are directed to Iran.

Control of the creek

There must be few ports in the world where the casual visitor can stroll unhindered among the ships and their wares, where piles of goods are left stacked and unguarded for days on an open and public quay; where one can take photographs to one's heart's content, chat to the sailors, and even climb up onto the boats for a glass of sweet tea. It looks like the most amazing free-for-all in the history of navigation.

Yet in fact, this is not so. It comes almost as a surprise that dhows using the creek and Hamriya are subject to the same checks and controls as in any port of the world, though rapidly and unobtrusively carried out here. A few can always be seen, tied up in the creek alongside the customs building near the Dubai fishmarket. There they must call to get all their paperwork in order, and to have their cargoes searched for any unwelcome contraband. The Dubai authorities keep a close eye on activities on their own back doorstep.

Dubai is also continuing its efforts to improve facilities in the creek. In the early days of the creek's expansion, a number of engineering works were established along its banks. Largest of these was the big McDermott yard beside the Maktoum Bridge. There whole oil rigs were constructed, and floated down the creek on their way to the sea. On the other shore, the IMS yard brought in large ships for repair, and kept a fleet of their own ships moored in between times. These heavy users of the creek were great contributors to Dubai's prosperity, but did little to enhance the environment, and created a hazard for dhows entering and leaving the creek. In the mid-1980s the McDermott yard was moved to Jebel Ali, and the IMS yard was soon scheduled to follow suit.

By the early 1990s pressure on space along the wharves for the dhows was becoming critical. Dhows were moored five or six abreast, which meant that goods being loaded and unloaded must be hauled across four or five other boats before reaching the outer one. So the construction of a large, four-basin dhow marina was undertaken on the site of the old McDermott yard, beside the bridge. The marina, designed to take 100 dhows at a time along its wharves, will relieve the pressure on the quays along the city front, enabling boats to moor just one or two abreast.

Happily for Dubai these dhows, which make the character of the place, will remain welcome within her creek. As an official publication has it, their movements within Hamriya Port and Dubai Creek are "a reliable reflection of the health of the entrepot trade."

The biggest ships

Today tankers are the biggest ships in the world, and these supertankers were created primarily to collect oil from the Gulf. These monster ships are divided into two classes. The commoner ones are the VLCCs (Very Large Crude Carriers), which weigh up to 350,000 deadweight tonnes. Such ships cost around $100 million to build and there are over 400 of them afloat around the world today. They are expected to have a lifespan of 15 to 20 years. The most popular size nowadays is between 250,000 and 280,000 deadweight tonnes.

Tankers even larger than these were built in the 1970s and early 1980s when oil prices were high. These ships are called ULCCs (Ultra Large Crude Carriers) and 65 of them now sail the seas. The biggest of them all is the Jahre Viking, built in Japan in 1976. This ship was previously called 'Happy Giant' and then 'Seawise Giant'. She was lengthened in 1980, damaged in 1988 in the 'tanker war', and then renamed the 'Jahre Viking' by her new Norwegian owners.

Tankers have today become some of the commonest ships in the Gulf. Their huge bulk makes them the most noticeable also, as they lie at anchor off the major ports along the Gulf coasts, or load from the terminals beside the oil rigs on the offshore oilfields. Some 3,000 tankers visit the Gulf each year, and on any given day there are around a hundred oil tankers afloat there. Many more are also waiting off the eastern coast of the UAE, before entering the Gulf to collect their loads, a habit acquired during the troubled times of the Iran-Iraq war.

At that time, in the mid-1980s, the vulnerability of large oil tankers was dramatically demonstrated during the so-called 'tanker war', when both sides attacked oil tankers calling at the terminals of the other side. Despite all the efforts made to protect them, some 550 merchant ships were hit by rockets and mines during these years, and most of them were oil tankers. Dramatic pictures of flaming oil tankers appeared in the world's press.

***A VLCC enters the docks in Dubai, assisted by tugs.
(Courtesy Dubai Dry Docks)***

Oil rigs in Gulf waters supply the tankers.
(Courtesy Crescent Petroleum)

Combating pollution

These pictures focussed attention on the problems of pollution associated with the transport of oil. An accident to most merchant ships results in the loss of a cargo which is bewailed by the owner and the insurance company, but beyond which nothing more is heard. Damage to an oil tanker, however, can result in millions of barrels of oil spilling out into the sea and coating beaches for many kilometres along the neighbouring coasts. Damage to marine and coastal life can also be severe.

So research has concentrated on ways in which oil tankers might be made more leak-proof, in the event of an accident. In the late 1980s discussions began in the International Maritime Organisation, and in individual countries of which the USA took the lead. Meanwhile tanker owners were reluctant to order new tankers which they feared might not comply with regulations that they knew must soon come into force. And indeed, in 1990 the USA introduced a ruling that all new tankers calling at American terminals must have double hulls. This was followed by a 1992 ruling of the IMO that by 1996 tankers worldwide must either have double hulls, or some other means of limiting leakage, such as a horizontal 'mid-deck' dividing the tank in two.

A double hull, which has a three-metre gap between the two shells of the hull, gives greater protection against piercing, though a powerful collision could still breach both hulls, and gas may build up between the two and cause explosions. A double-hulled tanker will also cost some 20 per cent to 30 per cent more than a single-hulled one.

The horizontal mid deck works on a different principle, depending on the fact that oil is lighter than water. The upper tank would be kept only part full, so that if the lower tank were breached there would be suction of oil into the upper tank as water entered the lower one.

Oddly, the same principle was practised in Dubai back in 1969, when its oil storage tanks were first positioned at the offshore field. These great khazans were designed like huge bells, the oil being kept in place in them by pressure from the water below.

Some three or four tankers a week call at Dubai Petroleum Company's offshore field. It is a convenient port of call for Gulf tankers, especially for those wishing to top up their loads, since the khazans stand in deep water. Here tankers can take on their maximum load before sailing away through the deep waters of the Strait of Hormuz, something they cannot do so easily in the shallower waters further up the Gulf.

Dry docks

The 'tanker war' brought suddenly into prominence a number of dry docks which had been built in the Gulf during the 1970s. They had faced initial

83

A second port

Back in the 1970s, however, with dozens of ships still waiting offshore, Sheikh Rashid had decided that more radical measures were needed if Dubai was to provide rapid berthing facilities for all ships calling here, both now and in the future. In 1975 he called his experts out to the barren shore near a little hill known as Jebel Ali and announced that a new port was to be built there. The port was to be a large one, such that no ship would ever have to wait offshore of Dubai again.

Sheikh Rashid had been much impressed by the Port of Antwerp which he had visited shortly before, and which seemed a good model to follow. This new port in Dubai was to be primarily an industrial port as well as ensuring that every ship that called would have a berth available. It would also be not far from the projected future capital of the UAE, which according to the provisional constitution was to be built on the borders of Abu Dhabi and Dubai.

So the amazing undertaking of the development of the Jebel Ali complex began. The two great basins of the harbour were dug out and a 16 kilometre-long deep-water channel was dredged out to sea, to allow safe and easy access to the harbour mouth. The harbour has 175,000 square metres of open storage space and a large number of Dutch barns

Jebel Ali provides facilities for laying up tankers.

and sheds for covered storage. It is surrounded by a 100 square-kilometre Free Zone and industrial complex. Sheikh Rashid gave this complex an initial boost by commissioning construction there of three large-scale industries: the aluminium smelter — Dubal, the gas plant — Dugas, and the power station. Jebel Ali Port itself was opened by Her Majesty, Queen Elizabeth II, during her visit to Dubai in 1979.

The harbour itself, with 67 berths in its two huge basins, is the largest man-made harbour in the world and was built at a cost of $2.5 billion. It can take the biggest ships afloat and will serve Dubai's needs for as far into the future as anyone can foresee. Here too the port's container terminal has become more and more busy over recent years. By 1990 five cranes were operating on its 1,300 metre-long container quay; the following year Jebel Ali Port handled nearly half-a-million TEU containers (Twenty-foot Equivalent Units — a 40-foot container counts as two TEUs).

The port caters comfortably for the needs of the large number of industrial units which have set up shop in the Jebel Ali Free Zone, and whose numbers exceeded 650 companies by the mid-1990s. These companies are attracted by the package of incentives which the Free Zone has to offer which includes one hundred per cent foreign ownership, a guaranteed 15-year tax holiday after start-up, repatriation of profits, and an excellent infrastructure.

Aerial view of Jebel Ali Port.

Dubai Ports Authority

Management of both Dubai's ports is run from the Jebel Ali headquarters of DPA and JAFZA.

Until 1991 Dubai's two ports were under separate and competing management. Both ports were expanding their operations very rapidly and it was decided that a more rational way of handling the ports would be to place them under the same management. As a result, the Dubai Ports Authority was inaugurated in May, 1991, with its head office at Jebel Ali.

In November of that year the Ports Authority celebrated a watershed in the work of the ports, the handling in one year of one million TEU containers. Almost 4,000 vessels had called at Dubai during the year, of which some 800 were container ships and 400 were oil tankers. This paved the way for continuing expansion in their activities in the future. In 1991 six new cranes were ordered, three for each port, as a measure of the Authority's confidence in the future of these outstanding harbours. By the end of 1993 the ports had handled 1.68 million TEUs, further consolidating DPA's position among the world's top 15 container ports.

Ships come into Dubai from all around the world, though her major suppliers are from India and the Far East, very much as trade into the Gulf has always been. The leading supply ports today are Singapore and Hong Kong, followed by Karachi and Bombay.

From the west, Wilmington, Hamburg and London all just make it into the top ten ports of origin. Trade leaving Dubai goes out in the opposite direction, with the main ports of destination for her exports or re-exports being within the Gulf — Bandar Abbas, Dammam, Kuwait and Bahrain heading the list. Karachi, Singapore and Bombay all feature also in the top ten destination ports.

An interesting element of Dubai's cargo handling has been provided by the opening at Dubai International Airport of the freight-handling Air Cargo Village. Sea/air cargo is a rapidly growing sector which offers considerable flexibility and economies of time and cost for importers and exporters alike. Goods which come into Dubai from Japan by sea, for example, and continue their journey from there onwards to Germany by air, would save a third of the journey time involved in an all-sea route, and 40 per cent of the costs of an all-air journey.

Meanwhile both Jebel Ali and Port Rashid still serve Dubai's traditional customers, the dhows which cluster so densely in Hamriya Port and the Creek. Some of these dhows also call in at Port Rashid and Jebel Ali, both for loading and unloading, thus forging a strong link between these huge modern harbours and Dubai's traditional trading heritage.

The control tower of Jebel Ali harbour.

from the struggles with ropes and sails, the race presents a scene of peace and silent beauty, quite different from present-day seafaring.

The sailing races are not the only wooden boat races currently gaining in popularity in the UAE. Even stranger craft take to the water for the longboat rowing races, also restricted to nationals. For these races, which again follow an old tradition, very long open boats set with rows and rows of seats, are rowed by some 90 oarsmen at a time. They must reflect the days when men strained at their oars in the galleys, but today the effort is willingly undertaken for the reward again consists of substantial prizes.

A third kind of wooden racing boat is also to be seen around the fishing harbours, the smallest and sleekest of them all. These are the little dhows which are raced with a pair of powerful outboard motors at the stern, dhows which reflect very closely the open wooden fishing boats in universal use until fibreglass boats filled the harbours. The old fishing boats can still be seen, beached around the edge of the water and often abandoned. The new racing versions are much faster — dangerous boats to handle at high speed in any but a calm sea — but very popular with the young today. Races for these boats are tightly organised with strict safety regulations, including crash helmets for the crews.

While all these races are for the local people, sons of Sindbad by inheritance, Dubai and the UAE are also acquiring a growing reputation internationally as a great place for water sports of all descriptions. The warm seas and long coastlines lend themselves to a wide variety of sports, from water skiing and wind surfing to jet skiing, from sports fishing to sailing of international standards. Above all, Dubai's powerboat races attract top competitors and their craft from all over the world.

The Gulf, which for thousands of years has been a much disputed highway, the route of tough maritime trading, is today drawing foreigners of all nationalities to its coasts, simply for the pleasure of the sport it offers. Sun, sand and sea here combine to produce a sportsman's paradise.

Sailing is popular with expatriates too.

Wooden power boat races provide another attraction.

Nearly 100 rowers man a longboat.

AUTHOR

Shirley Kay first came to the Gulf in 1968, when she spent three years in Bahrain, with spells in Dubai and Muscat. She returned in 1985 to Dubai, where her husband was appointed British Consul General.

She first acquired an interest in Arab seafaring while living in Bahrain in a house on the beach. A palm-frond fish trap ran out to sea from the beach and was regularly visited by fishermen. Her own small sailing boat, kept on the same beach, enabled her to observe Arab craft at close quarters. Exciting archaeological discoveries in the Gulf at the time showed that seafaring was no new venture, that maritime trading there was more than 5,000 years old.

Shirley Kay studied languages at Cambridge University, Arabic at Shemlan in the Lebanon, and Middle Eastern archaeology at the Institute of Archaeology in London. This is her eighth book in the Arabian Heritage Series and 15th on the Middle East as a whole. She has made some 30 documentary films for Dubai Television, many of which are available as Arabian Heritage videos.

ACKNOWLEDGEMENTS

Of the many people who have helped me, I should particularly like to thank Neville Allen for his beautiful old photographs, and United Colour Film Professional Division for supplying and processing much of my film. Hassan Al Fardan allowed me to photograph his pearls, and Muhammed bin Thani his pearling dhow.

For tankers, I am indebted to Charlotte Haviland of John Swire & Sons, Robert Shipman of Harley Mullion, Petro-Logistics Ltd of Geneva, and Andrew Craig Bennett of Charles Taylor & Co; on the history of Dubai port and creek, to Captain Arthur Jarman, Captain William Nelson and Dick Denning; and on dhow building, to Obaid bin Saloom, Obaid bu Khasham and Saeed Isa Bushhab. Once again the Abu Dhabi Centre for Documentation and Research proved an invaluable source of research material. Thanks also to Roohi Ali Khan and Karen Coutinho of Motivate Publishing.

Above all, I am extremely grateful to Sultan bin Sulayem and the Dubai Ports Authority, whose support and sponsorship have made possible the publication of this book.

BIBLIOGRAPHY

Barbosa, D:
The Book of Duarte Barbosa, 1518, reprint 1967.

Bibby, G:
Looking for Dilmun, 1969.

Dawood, N J (trans):
Tales from The Thousand and One Nights, 1973.

Hawkins, C W:
The Dhow, 1977.

Heyerdahl, T:
The Tigris Expedition, 1980.

Hourani, G F:
Arab Seafaring, 1963.

Howarth, D:
Dhows, 1977.

Khalifa, H A & Rice M (eds):
Bahrain Through the Ages, 1986.

Martin, E B & C P:
Cargoes of the East, 1978.

Ministry of Culture, Oman:
Oman, a Seafaring Nation, 1979.

Schoff, W H (trans):
The Periplus of the Erythraean Sea, 1911, reprint 1974.

Severin, T:
The Sindbad Voyage, 1982.

Strabo:
Geography XVI, reprint 1966.

Villiers, A J:
Sons of Sindbad, 1940, reprint 1969.

Williamson, A:
"Hormuz and the trade of the Gulf in the 14th and 15th centuries AD" in *Proceedings of the Seminar for Arabian Studies,* 1972.

INDEX

Arabian Profiles
edited by Ian Fairservice and Chuck Grieve

Land of the Emirates
by Shirley Kay

Enchanting Oman
by Shirley Kay

Bahrain – Island Heritage
by Shirley Kay

Kuwait – A New Beginning
by Gail Seery

Dubai – Gateway to the Gulf
edited by Ian Fairservice

Abu Dhabi – Garden City of the Gulf
by Peter Hellyer and Ian Fairservice

Sharjah – Heritage and Progress
by Shirley Kay

Fujairah – An Arabian Jewel
by Peter Hellyer

Portrait of Ras Al Khaimah
by Shirley Kay

Gulf Landscapes
by Elizabeth Collas and Andrew Taylor

Birds of Southern Arabia
by Dave Robinson and Adrian Chapman

Falconry and Birds of Prey in the Gulf
by Dr David Remple and Christian Gross

The Living Desert
by Marycke Jongbloed

Seashells of Southern Arabia
by Donald and Eloise Bosch

The Living Seas
by Frances Dipper and Tony Woodward

Mammals of the Southern Gulf
by Christian Gross

Seafarers of the Gulf
by Shirley Kay

Architectural Heritage of the Gulf
by Shirley Kay and Dariush Zandi

Emirates Archaeological Heritage
by Shirley Kay

Sketchbook Arabia
by Margaret Henderson

Storm Command
by General Sir Peter de la Billière

This Strange Eventful History
by Edward Henderson

Juha – Last of the Errant Knights
by Mustapha Kamal,
translated by Jack Briggs

Fun in the Emirates
by Aisha Bowers and Leslie P Engelland

Fun in the Gulf
by Aisha Bowers and Leslie P Engelland

Mother Without a Mask
by Patricia Holton

Zelzelah – A Woman Before Her Time
by Mariam Behnam

Premier Editions

A Day Above Oman
by John Nowell

Forts of Oman
by Walter Dinteman

Land of the Emirates
by Shirley Kay

MOTIVATE
PUBLISHING

Abu Dhabi – Garden City of the Gulf
edited by Ian Fairservice and Peter Hellyer

50 Great Curries of India
by Camellia Panjabi

The Thesiger Library

Written and photographed
by Wilfred Thesiger:

Arabian Sands
The Marsh Arabs
Desert, Marsh and Mountain
My Kenya Days

The Thesiger Collection
a catalogue of photographs
by Wilfred Thesiger

Thesiger's Return
by Peter Clark
with photographs by Wilfred Thesiger

Arabian Heritage Guides

Snorkelling and Diving in Oman
by Rod Salm and Robert Baldwin

The Green Guide to the Emirates
by Marycke Jongbloed

**Off-Road in the Emirates
Volumes 1 & 2**
by Dariush Zandi

Off-Road in Oman
by Heiner Klein and Rebecca Brickson

Beachcombers' Guide to the Gulf
by Tony Woodward

Spoken Arabic – Step-by-Step
by John Kirkbright

Arabian Albums

Written and photographed
by Ronald Codrai:

Dubai – An Arabian Album

Abu Dhabi – An Arabian Album

**The North-East Shaikhdoms –
An Arabian Album**